30 Day Mind-Work Project
30 days of Renewing, Rejuvenating, Reprogramming

By
Starla C. Quinn

For more information and other resource materials, please visit: majestywomensacademy.com

Introduction

It is such a blessing that you have decided to take the course and do something great for your mind and ultimately your life. To live the abundant life God created us to live, we must be right in our thinking and our words. The way we think and what we speak determines how we live. With right thinking, we produce right actions that unlock the doors to so many of our blessings. Faith is present in right thinking, and without it, nothing is possible. Coming to the fullness of everything God ever knew you could do, be and have is not possible without faith and a positive mind. 30 Day Mind-Work Project gives you 30 days of study to equip your mind and get your thinking on the right track. There is an itinerary of study for each day of the project. Scheduled reading devotions, joining scriptures, and exercises are all based on God's principles. Being able to reprogram our minds to think the way God intended will produce marvelous results in our lives and our circumstances. Thanks for joining the project! Let's get started.

Blessings!

Day 1
You Are What You Think

"For as he thinketh in his heart, so is he…"

-Proverbs 23:7 (KJV)

What you think – you become. Whatever you think about long enough, consumes you, and everything else becomes irrelevant. We must guard ourselves by protecting our minds against the forces that seek to still, kill, and destroy our purpose – our lives. We have no control over the attempts that are made against us, but we have total control over what we choose to allow access to our minds. The world will temp us to worry and meditate on our lack and imperfections until they have consumed us. The way we see ourselves and our lives should be no different than the way God sees us – nothing missing, nothing broken. You must, at all times, know who you are in Christ, otherwise, the world will define you. You must know that you are a part of the Creator and nothing less – Royalty. No matter what circumstances have led you to believe, what others have washed into your head, or what society wants you to believe, you are a divine creation of the Most High God, and you are chosen and equipped to do great things for the Kingdom!

~

Prayer

Dear Heavenly Father, I want to be all that You created me to be. And just as important, I want to know who I am in You and What I'm supposed to be. Grant me Godly wisdom, knowledge and understanding so that I may always know when I am harboring thoughts that seek to still, kill and destroy everything you have planned for me. Help me to always see myself the way you see me. Help me to discover my true beauty and identity in You. In everything, I give You thanks and praise for Who You are and whom You created me to be; In Jesus' Name, Amen.

Scriptures

Psalms 139:14

Ephesians 2:10

John 15: 5

Exercise

On several small pieces of paper, write down the following phrases and put them in places you visit often through the day. Having them as a constant reminder of who you are in Christ will keep your confidence in order:

I am fearfully and wonderfully made. (Psalm 139:14)

I am more precious than rubies; nothing compares to me. (Proverbs 3:15)

Day 2
The Mind of Christ

"Let this mind be in you, which was also in Christ Jesus…"

-Philippians 2:5 (KJV)

Having the mind of Christ changes the way we see ourselves and other situations. Jesus lived a life of complete faith. When He spoke, He believed what He said without a doubt as to whether or not a certain thing would happen. He instructs, throughout the Word, how to think and believe. Mark 11:24 says that if we believe what we have asked for in prayer and do not doubt, it is already done for us. The way we think produces actions that we will eventually carry out. When you think negatively about a situation, negative emotions that follow will cause you to look at your circumstance in a dim light. You will miss what God is trying to do in your life and the promise that everything will work out for your good. Discipline yourself to think the way Jesus inspired us to think, and you will find yourself living the way He intended for us to live – nothing missing – nothing broken.

~

Prayer

Dear God, I long to be more like You. Show me how to forsake the thoughts of the world so that I may think more like You. I want to live a life of total faith and trust in You; that I may become disciplined to Your ways and Your Will. Make me sensitive to Your voice so that I may know when I am off track in my thinking. Strengthen my mind so that I may make right choices and produce right behavior. Guard my mind against the forces that seek to lure me away from Your path. I give You my mind and my heart to do with as You please; for You know what is best for me; In Jesus' Name, Amen.

Scriptures

Mark 11:12 - 24

Philippians 4:6

Romans 12:2

Exercise

Replace negative thoughts with positive ones. Keep a notebook or journal with you. In it, write down something positive every day. Find the good in every situation – on purpose. When you are tempted to say something negative about yourself, a situation or someone else, find something positive to say instead. Think positive on purpose.

"Thou wilt keep him in perfect peace, whose mind is stayed on thee: because he trusteth in thee."
Isaiah 26:3 (KJV)

Day 3
True Power

"I can do all things through Christ Who strengthens me."

-Philippians 4:13 (KJ2000B)

       True power comes from God. The only way that we are able to have true, genuine power is through the One Who resides in us – Jesus Christ. Through Him, we are able to do anything. By having a personal relationship with God, we are allowed access to things we do not deserve and could never earn. He is well equipped to bring our deepest desires to the light. Through Him, we are able to live in abundance and in the overflow which has been made available to us through the finished work of Christ. Through Christ, our possibilities are endless. The power of God that is present in us when we allow Him to be the head of our lives gives us access to our hearts desires.

~

Prayer

Dear God, there is no other like You. I know that through You, I can do all things. Thank You for Your strength and power. Help me to always trust in You and allow You to lead me in every situation. I invite You to be the head of my life. I make You the King of my life, my heart and my mind. Empower me as I fall back and allow You to take the lead; In Jesus' Name, Amen.

Scriptures

Ephesians 3:16-19

Matthew 19:26

2 Corinthians 12:9-10

Exercise

Exercise your power. Talk to God before you make decisions. Allow Him to take the lead as you trust His answers and guidance. When He speaks, follow. Even when things don't always make sense, trust Him. Have faith that He is present and well able to bring about a good work in you. Consult Him first in everything, obey, and watch your life change for the better.

"Now unto him that is able to do exceeding abundantly above all that we ask or think, according to the power that worketh in us…"

Ephesians 3:20 (KJV)

Day 4
Seeing is Believing

"For we walk by faith, not by sight..."

-2 Corinthians 5:7 (KJV)

The manifestation of your blessings starts in your mind – your spiritual vision. You must see them being done before it actually shows up in your life. Believe that God has already answered your prayers as if He called you on the phone and said He was on the way. After you have prayed for something, go on living as though you have been approved. Mark 11:24 tells us that whatever we ask for in prayer, if we do not doubt in our hearts but believe that what we asked for has been done for us, we shall receive it. Be bold and go to God in prayer, then go on expecting those things, which you have prayed for, to manifest in your life. Remember that God's timing is perfect. So no matter how long it takes, keep believing and you will see it.

~

Prayer

Dear God, You have never failed me. You have proven Your word to be true. Give me the strength to hold on and keep believing, even in times when it doesn't seem as though anything is happening. I know that You will never forsake me. I trust You Lord; In Jesus' Name, Amen.

Scriptures

Psalms 46:10

Romans 10:17

Proverbs 3:5-6

Exercise

Write down your vision. Whatever you hope to see in your life and the prayers you've left with God, write it down in a notebook or journal. Prepare yourself to receive what you have prayed for, and expect it. Thank God in advance for answering your prayers and giving you the desires of your heart.

"Now faith is the substance of things hoped for, the evidence of things not seen…"
                              Hebrews 11: 1 (KJV)

"And all things, whatsoever ye shall ask in prayer, believing, ye shall receive."
                              Matthew 21:22 (KJV)

Day 5
God's Timing is Perfect

"And let us not be weary in well doing: for in due season we shall reap, if we faint not."

-Galatians 6:9 (KJV)

It's gonna happen! Whatever you've been praying and believing for, God is going to bring it to pass. No matter how shaky the ground gets or how uncertain the situation may seem, God is well able to do it. As the scripture above states, we will reap in due season if we don't give up. Keep praying, believing, trusting and expecting God to do miraculous things in your life. God is faithful and has never failed us. If He gave His only Son to die for us, what else wouldn't He do? Everything else is easy. Just know that God wants you to have the desires of your heart as well as what is best for you. God works in and out of time, so running out of time is not an option here. When it seems as though God didn't come in time, remember that He has a plan, even if we cannot see it just yet. Trust Him. In the scriptures, Jesus allowed people to remain dead for 3 days before resurrecting them; He wanted to show that there is no amount of time or situation that can Keep Him from doing just what He said He'd do. All you have to do is believe.

~

Prayer

Dear God, I know that we will never be disappointed when we wait on You. You have never failed us. Your timing is perfect, and in Your time, I believe that You will grant me the desires of my heart. I trust that You have already gone to work on my behalf. Give me patience to stand firmly planted on Your word and on Your promise as You work things out for me. Help me to not get in Your way or mess things up by trying to answer my own prayers and solve my own problems. Thank You for Your best and all that You have done on Your time; You know what is best for me. In Jesus' Name, Amen.

Scriptures

Hebrews 11:6

Ecclesiastes 8:6

Isaiah 40:31

Exercise

Write down what you are praying and believing God to do in your life. Then give thanks for those things as though He has already done them. Count your blessings every day by thanking God for something that He has already done in your life as you wait for Him to answer your prayers.

"For the vision [is] yet for an appointed time, but at the end, it shall speak and not lie: though it tarry, wait for it; because it will surely come, it will not tarry."
Habakkuk 2:3 (KJV)

Day 6
Faith over Fear

"I sought the Lord, and He heard me, and delivered me from all my fears."

-Psalms 34:4 (KJV)

Trust God and believe that He is always there, no matter the circumstance, to see you through. There is no place you can go that God can't find you and deliver just as He has promised. His Word says that He will never leave nor forsake us, and He stands firm on His Word. Be bold and stand firmly on God's promise to keep you. There is nothing you cannot do through Christ Who strengthens you (Philippians 4:13). There is nothing that He cannot fix, no problem He cannot solve, no pain He cannot heal, no burden He cannot bear and no prayer He cannot answer. There is nothing and no one greater than God. Refuse to be moved by trials and tribulations. Cancel out fear by going forward and believing even though a solution doesn't seem likely. Whenever fear presents itself and tries to keep you from doing something, grab your faith and do it anyway, knowing that God is standing in you. Stand firmly on His Word as you believe that He is a very present help in your times of need.

~

Prayer

Heavenly Father, I come before You with my heart in my hands; Encourage it and teach me to be strong and of good courage. I rest firmly on Your promise to never leave nor forsake me. You have never failed me and have promised to be there in my times of trouble. I cast my cares upon You so that You may care for me, as You have promised in Your word. Remind me that I can do anything through You. I am comforted by the truth that there is nothing to hard for You. Cover me with a double portion of Your peace; In Jesus' Name, Amen.

Scriptures

2 Timothy 1:7

1 John 4:18

Psalms 56:3-4

Exercise

Do it afraid. Step out on faith and do some things you have wanted to do but talked yourself out of them due to fear of what people think or fear of failing. Knock down fear in every direction of your life by tackling them one by one.

"Go in the direction of fear and you will find success there also."
    -Starla C. Quinn (Author, Speaker, Life coach, Entrepreneur)

"Fear thou not; for I [am] with thee: be not dismayed; for I [am] thy God: I will strengthen thee; yea, I will help thee; yea, I will uphold thee with the right hand of my righteousness.
                                    Isaiah 41:10 (KJV)

Day 7
Ask and You Shall Receive

"Ask and it will be given to you; seek and you will find; knock and the door will be opened to you."

-Matthew 7:7 (NIV)

God hears and honors our prayers. Mark 11:24 tells us that we will receive what we ask for in prayer if we do not doubt but believe that it will be done for us. One of the things that pleases God is to grant us the desires of our hearts and that we live in abundance. When we pray, He goes to work on what we have asked of Him. Our job of believing can be hindered by our circumstances and the people around us. We must believe, no matter what, that God has gone before us to do what only He can do. Sometimes we don't recognize our answered prayers because it didn't come exactly the way we asked, but God has our best interest at heart. You can rest assured that however God decides to honor our request will be better than anything that we could have ever imagined or wanted for ourselves. Ask and trust that God will honor your prayers. Keep an open heart and expect God to move in a major way!

~

Prayer

Lord, I know that You know what is best for me. I know that it pleases You to grant the desires of my heart. I believe that Your word is true, and I trust You to do what only You can. Give me the strength to hold on to my faith regardless of my circumstances and what others around me want me to believe. I choose to believe in You. You will never leave me or forsake me. I will lean on Your word and stand on Your promise as I expect a move from You in my favor. Thank You Father; In Jesus' Name; Amen.

Scriptures

Matthew 21:22

John 14:13-14

Philippians 4:6-8

Exercise

Cancel out any bit of doubt by believing that God will answer your prayers. When you feel doubt creeping in, stop yourself from meditating on it and speak out loud. Declare this: No! I believe God, and He cannot lie. He will do just as He said.

"If ye abide in me, and my words abide in you, ye shall ask what ye will, and it shall be done unto you." (John 15:7)

"And this is the confidence that we have in Him, that, if we ask anything according to His will, He heareth us:" (1 John 5:14)

Day 8
The Chosen One

"For many are called, but few are chosen."

-Matthew 22:14 (NLV)

You have a purpose and were called and ordained by God to do great things. Your gifts are needed to elevate the kingdom of God and bring Him glory. When we allow God to be the head of our lives and lead us in all that we do, we will find ourselves living in abundance and accomplishing our dreams. There is no gift too small or insignificant that God cannot use for His glory and your good. God placed something on the inside of us that will sustain us if we follow His plan. Everything you've gone through was for a special moment where you would become everything that He ever knew you could be. All the pain, heartache and sleepless nights were strengthening you and preparing you for your purpose. Embrace the things that you learned during your trials and tribulations. Take action and begin using your gifts for the kingdom. Pray and ask God to show you the way. You were destined to do great and marvelous things!

~

Prayer

Lord, show me the way. Show me how to use all that I am for Your glory. I want to become all that You have created me to be. Help me see the beauty that was created in the darkness. Use me as You will. Uncover all of the hidden gems that You have placed in me, and give me the strength to use them. Open doors that will allow me to use my gifts to elevate and increase Your kingdom; In Jesus' Name; Amen.

Scriptures

1 Peter 2:9

Colossians 3:12-17

Deuteronomy 14:2

Exercise

Write down your gifts and passions. Then, think of and write down ways that you can use these things to glorify the kingdom of God. Pray for God to give you ideas, and then act on them.

"A person's gift opens doors for him, bringing him access to important people." Proverbs 18:16 (ISV)

"And we know that God causes all things to work together for good to those who love God, to those who are called according to His purpose." (Romans 8:28)

Day 9
Unexpected Blessings

"Every good and perfect gift is from above, coming down from the Father of the heavenly lights, who does not change like shifting shadows."

- James 1:17 (NIV)

Expect a move from God. No matter how difficult the situation may seem, God is always ready to move on your behalf in a moments notice. There is nowhere you can go where God can't find you and bless you. When you pray, God goes before you to do what only He can and make things happen for you. Even when we can't see God working, He is. His silence doesn't mean there is no activity going on. Just as we cannot see roots growing underground; we go out one day and there's a tree. Trust that God is moving in ways that you cannot see at this point. Soon, everything that He is doing on your behalf will be revealed. When you least expect it, all of the blessings that you've been praying for will be bestowed upon you. Hold on to His word and be firmly planted on His promise. Keep praying and believing. Keep your eyes on the King and expect Him to do mighty things.

~

Prayer

Lord, thank You for going before me and working things out for me. I am leaning on Your word and standing on Your promise. Do what only You can do and encourage my heart while I am waiting on You. Cover me in Your peace when I become impatient. Give me the strength to not grow weary as I wait patiently on You. And because I know that Your word is true, I give You thanks, now, before I see the manifestation of all that You are doing in my life and on my behalf; In Jesus' Name; Amen.

Scriptures

Luke 6:38

2 Corinthians 9:8

Philippians 2:13

Exercise

Give thanks to God for the things that He is doing on your behalf. Even if you cannot see what He is doing at this stage, be thankful in advance. Giving thanks is the driving force that will propel your blessings to you faster. Acknowledge God every step of the way.

"Beloved, I wish above all things that thou mayest prosper and be in health, even as thy soul prospereth." (3 John 1:2)

"The LORD bless thee, and keep thee…" (Numbers 6:24-26)

Day 10
The Power of Prayer

"If you believe, you will receive whatever you ask in prayer."

-Matthew 21:22 (NIV)

Something wonderful happens when we pray. The power of God goes to work in us and in our circumstances. Through prayer, you can make your request known to the Father Who will grant your request. When we pray, we are able to cast our cares and share our hearts with God. In return, He speaks to us and encourages our hearts. The power of God is released into our lives when we pray. His favor and anointing covers us and allows us to have things that we could never obtain ourselves. Being faithful and developing a regular prayer life keeps us near to God and the power that comes from only Him. If you haven't already, make prayer a regular part of your daily life and watch God move in your life in a major way. Prayer changes things!

~

Prayer

Father, I am thankful that I can come to You in prayer. It is through prayer that I am able to make my request known and cast my cares. You carry away my burdens and give me strength to endure when I am going through. Your power strengthens me. I will remain confident knowing that You hear my prayers and will grant the desires of my heart at the right time. And I know that Your timing is perfect; In Jesus' Name; Amen.

Scriptures

Matthew 7:7

Mark 9:29

Ephesians 6:18

Exercise

Make time to pray everyday. Find a quiet place and spend some time talking to God. Make prayer a part of your everyday life.

"Whatever you ask in My name, this I will do, that the Father may be glorified in the Son. If you ask Me anything in My name, I will do it. (John 14:13-14)

"Don't pray when you feel like it. Have an appointment with the Lord and keep it. A man is powerful on his knees."

-Corrie ten Boom (1892-1983)

Day 11
Let Go And Let God

"Hold everything in your hands lightly, otherwise it hurts when God pries your fingers open."

-Corrie ten Boom (1892-1983)

Worrying about our problems never provided a solution. Instead, worrying prolongs our problems while creating more problems, such as messing things up by trying to solve our own problems and answer our own prayers. Answers to our prayers are derived in faith and trusting God to do what He has promised; worrying shows that we do not trust that God will answer. Fear is a partner of worry and cancels out our faith — Fear that our circumstances will get the best of us, and that there will be no end to our suffering. We must trust God no matter what. Let go and let God do what only He can do. We have to be brave enough to cast our cares into our Father's hands and trust that He will carry them for us while delivering a solution in His own time. His timing is nothing less than perfect, and He will answer. Be patient. Rest in the promise that God will never leave nor forsake us, and He has never failed us. Keep praying, trusting and believing that God has a perfect plan!

~

Prayer

Father, forgive me for not fully believing in Your word. I know that You will never leave nor forsake me. You have never failed me. I trust You to do what only You can. I cast my cares upon You. Cover me in Your peace while I wait patiently on You. Your timing is perfect, and I know that You will provide a solution in due time. Comfort me while I wait. Thank You for Your truth and faithfulness to Your word; In Jesus' Name; Amen.

Scriptures

Matthew 6:25-34

Isaiah 26:3

Psalms 23:1-6

Exercise

Write down whatever worries you have. Then, one-by-one, pray and ask God to take those worries and, in turn, provide an answer. Pray for peace. After you give your problems to God, leave them there; Walk away confident in the Lord; Rest knowing that He is working on a solution.

"Never be afraid to trust an unknown future to a known God."
                                        -Corrie ten Boom (1892-1983)

"Worry does not empty tomorrow of its sorrow, it empties today of its strength."

                                        -Corrie ten Boom (1892-1983)

Day 12
Forgiveness

"Be kind to one another, tenderhearted, forgiving one another, as God in Christ forgave you."

-Ephesians 4:32 (ESV)

Unforgiveness keeps you from receiving all that God wants to do in your life. No matter how badly you were hurt or offended, grudges only bring more hurt. Don't allow your heart to be hardened by the things that may have occurred. Pray and ask God to help you to forgive. When the chance to forgive arises, take it. Don't miss an opportunity to get right with yourself and with God. Create moments to show forgiveness against those who have somehow wronged you. When you forgive, it is for you – not them. It allows the dark past that hinders your blessings to be lifted. Don't allow unforgiveness to steal everything that God wants to do in your life. Let love be the driving force that cast out anger and strife. Forgive those that have wronged you just as our heavenly Father forgave and continues to forgive us. Extend your hand of forgiveness and watch your life move in ways you never imagined!

~

Prayer

Lord, forgive me for harboring unforgiveness in my heart. You teach us everyday that we should forgive one another just as You forgave us. Give me the strength to let go of the anger and pain that rents space in my mind and in my heart. Don't allow unforgiveness to steal everything You want to do in my life. I want to be more like You Father – able to forgive and show love to those who have wronged me. I thank You for Your mercy, grace and Forgiveness, and for giving me the strength to forgive; In Jesus' Name; Amen

Scriptures

Mark 11:25

Matthew 6:14-15

1 John 4:20

Exercise

Choose to forgive. Write down every situation or person that you have not forgiven; this could even be yourself. Once they've been written, pray and ask God to give you the strength to forgive. Place your hand on each one and picture God reaching down and taking the hurt, pain, and anger away. See them forgiven on purpose.

"The weak can never forgive. Forgiveness is the attribute of the strong."

-Mahatma Gandhi (1869-1948)

Day 13
Saved By Grace

"For it is by grace you have been saved, through faith—and this is not from yourselves, it is the gift of God--"

-Ephesians 2:8 (NIV)

I remember the days I spent walking the tight rope—trying to do everything just right—so that God would answer my prayers. I figured if I failed at being perfect, my prayers wouldn't pass the ceiling. I drove myself insane counting the sins in my cup everyday. I got so tired of re-repenting that I gave up all together. There was no way I could keep up with perfect. But that is where the beauty happened. It was when I gave up that God said, "It's about time. I was waiting for you to realize that there is nothing for you to do except believe." I realized that His grace was sufficient. I found that I could never earn God's blessings and answers to my prayers. Grace would allow me to have them undeservingly through the finished work of Christ on Calvary. The miracle happened when I realized that I am saved by grace through faith!

~

Prayer

Father, I am so thankful for Your grace that covers me. I am not deserving of all the things You have done and continue to do for me, and I know that I could never earn them. Thank You for loving me in spite of me. Touch my mind so that I always remember that it is Your grace that covers me and that my only job is to believe; In Jesus' Name; Amen.

Scriptures

2 Corinthians 12:9

Romans 11:6

Numbers 6:25

Exercise

Share the grace of God with others. Look for opportunities to extend grace to someone as Christ has done for us. There may be times when we feel as though our children or others aren't deserving of our gifts, but extend the hand of grace and bless them anyway.

"And from His fullness we have all received, grace upon grace."
John 1: 16 (ESV)

"You then, my child, be strengthened by the grace that is in Christ Jesus…" *2 Timothy 2:1 (ESV)*

Day 14
Giving Thanks

"Give thanks in all circumstances; for this is the will of God in Christ Jesus for you."

-1 Thessalonians 5:18 (ESV)

I used to complain about my circumstances, and it always seemed that I was always looking for more. What I had wasn't good enough – until I lost what I had. It wasn't until then that I realized that I was complaining about a situation that could have been much worse. There were people who were going through worse. I witnessed a family who barely had anything at all, yet, they were grateful and happy. It taught me to count those little blessings that often go unnoticed. I quickly changed my attitude toward all that God had done in my life and learned to appreciate and give thanks for what I had. I thanked God through my trials, knowing that He was using them to do a good work in me. When you give God thanks for what you have, in spite of your current situation or circumstance, you allow His blessings to come quickly. In order to receive more, we must first be genuinely thankful for the things that we have. Count your blessings. There are things around you that someone else is praying for. Learn to be content where you are with what you have, and you will see blessings fall like never before!

~

Prayer

God, forgive me for the blessings that I take for granted and the things that I have overlooked. You have done great things in my life. No matter how small, I am grateful for all that You have done in my life and everything that You are doing right now, at this very moment. Thank You Father for all the ways that You have made for me and the paths that You are clearing on my behalf. If you never do anything else for me, You have done more than enough. I could spend all of eternity thanking You for all that You have done and still need more time. Thank You Lord; In Jesus' Name; Amen.

Scriptures

Hebrews 13:15

Psalm 136:1-26

1 Chronicles 29:12-14

Exercise

Count your blessings. Each day find something to be thankful for. Let your praises be known to God. When you are tempted to complain, look for the good instead and give thanks. Keep a journal of thanks where you can continue to count your blessings and record your thanks. There is something to be thankful for in every situation; look for it.

"And now we thank You, our God, and praise Your glorious name."   *1 Chronicles 29:13 (ESV)*

Day 15
Mind Work

"You will keep him in perfect peace whose mind is stayed on you, because he trusts in you."

-Isaiah 26:3 (ESV)

Peace comes from trusting God and relying firmly on His word. The more of His word you have, the better equipped you are to deal with circumstances when they arise. The word of God is a shield that guards your mind against the lies and destruction of the enemy. Keep it near. Conditioning your mind to live by His word keeps you surrounded in His peace. Your abundance, peace, and overflow come from ingesting and working the word of God. Study His word and spend more time talking to God and allowing Him to speak to you. This guide is a great place to start. Keep these habits and set aside time to spend with God on a regular basis.

~

Prayer

Lord, cover me in Your peace. Help me to keep my mind stayed on You. I place my cares in Your hands, and I know that You care for me. I will trust You and Your word. When I become anxious, remind me that You are there. Show me how to stay in my place and not take on more than You have allowed me to bear. Remind me to never get ahead of You. Thank You, Father, for Your peace; In Jesus' Name; Amen.

Scriptures

2 Thessalonians 3:16

John 16:33

1 Peter 5:7

Exercise

Give it to Him. Cast your cares upon the Lord by praying and asking Him to grant you Godly peace. Turn all of your worries over to Him in prayer and leave them there. Walk away with a clear mind and open heart. Trust that God is going to cover you in His peace as you go through.

"Peace comes from within. Do not seek it without."
                    -Gautama Buddha (Sixth century B.C.)

"Each one has to find his peace from within. And peace to be real must be unaffected by outside circumstances."
                    -Mahatma Gandhi (1869-1948)

Day 16
The Anointing

"Plan and plant your gifts. Pray and play your role. The harvest is assured when God manifests His anointing power in your passionate actions."

-Israelmore Ayivor (Author)

You are anointed with the power of God to do great things. When we trust His anointing on our lives and step out on faith and use our gifts, God gets the glory. He anointed us For His glory, that we might roll our works over to Him and elevate His kingdom. We are rewarded richly when we realize that we have been anointed by God and then use our faith to go forth and do great things, knowing that the greater God that resides in us cannot fail. Stand tall and go boldly into your purpose. Do what God has called you to do and trust that He will never let you fall. You have been chosen and called to do great works for the kingdom. Against all circumstances, trust God and the anointing that covers you.

~

Prayer

Heavenly Father, thank You for Your anointing. Give me the strength and courage to go forth and do what You have anointed me to do. Show me the way. Lead me into my divine purpose so that I may become all that You have created me to be. I roll my works over to the kingdom. It is my desire to use all that I am to glorify You; In Jesus' Name; Amen.

Scriptures

Psalm 23:1-6

1 John 2:27

Luke 4:18

Exercise

What has God called you to do? Discover and use the gifts that God has put in you to glorify the kingdom. You have been anointed to do great things.

"But you have been anointed by the Holy One, and you all have knowledge."   *-1 John 2:20 (ESV)*

"Now it is God who makes both us and you stand firm in Christ. He anointed us…"   *-2 Corinthians 1:21 (NIV)*

Day 17
Abundant Harvest

"Before the fruits of prosperity can come, the storms of life need to first bring the required rains of testing, which mixes with the seeds of wisdom to produce a mature harvest."

-Lincoln Patz

There is no greater feeling than waking up hungry and realizing your harvest has come in. Whatever you are believing God to do in your life, He can do above and beyond just that. Infact, Ephesians 3:20 says that He can do infinitely more than we dare to ask, think or dream. Think Bigger. God will take what you are believing for and turn it into something that you can't even fathom. Our human mind cannot process how Big Our God is and what He can do. Trust His timing. Just because you can't see your harvest now doesn't mean there aren't roots sprouted underground. It's just a matter of time. When you least expect it, you will wake up one day to find your harvest has come in. Keep praying, believing, and preparing to receive.

~

Prayer

Heavenly Father, thank You for the blessings that You have bestowed upon me. I know that there is infinitely more that You want to do in my life. Encourage my heart as I wait patiently for You to deliver my harvest. I pray that I become sensitive to Your voice so that I may hear and follow Your instruction that puts me on the path of receiving. I believe that there are roots sprouting underground, and it is a matter of time before I see my abundant harvest; In Jesus' Name; Amen.

Scriptures

Deuteronomy 28:1-68

Psalm 72:16

Luke 6:38

Exercise

Sow in the direction of your harvest. Invest in the areas that you want to see sprout. Prepare for the harvest by including God in everything you do. Follow His instruction. Be ready to receive what God is about to do in your life.

"Everyone also to whom God has given wealth and possessions and power to enjoy them, and to accept his lot and rejoice in his toil—this is the gift of God."

-Ecclesiastes 5:19 (ESV)

Day 18
Rainbow Days

"I have set my rainbow in the clouds, and it will be the sign of the covenant between me and the earth."

-Genesis 9:13 (NIV)

From experience, I know that there are times when those grey clouds seem to rain on just you. But I am here to tell you that it won't be that way always. No matter what trials and circumstances temp you to believe, God will never let you drown in your problems. He put a rainbow in the sky as a covenant that says, no matter how much it rains, He will never again allow the earth to flood. This is great news for us as believers. No matter how saturated we get by our problems or how much they rise, God will be there to see us through. When the storms of life hit, take shelter in God and rely on His promise to rescue you. Trust Him. Your rainbow is coming!

~

Prayer

Lord, thank You for Your promise that You will never let me drown in my problems. Comfort me when I can't see a way out. Help me to find shelter in Your word when I am feeling lost and unsure. Shine Your light for me so that I can safely find my way. Encourage my heart while I wait for my rainbow; In Jesus' Name; Amen.

Scriptures

John 15:7-8

Psalm 37:4

2 Corinthians 1:20

Exercise

Write down this phrase on pieces of paper: My rainbow is coming! Then, put them up in places you visit often so that you will always be reminded of God's promise.

"For I know the plans I have for you, declares the Lord, plans for welfare and not for evil, to give you a future and a hope."

-Jeremiah 29: 11(ESV)

Day 19
Victory

"But thanks be to God, which giveth us the victory through our Lord Jesus Christ."

-1 Corinthians 15:57 (KJB)

The battle is not yours. No matter what your circumstance or how intense, there is nothing too hard for God. We can rest assured that He has already gone before us to fight our battles. All we have to do is rest in the promise that He has already done exactly what He said He will do. It is a matter of time before we see the manifestation of everything He is working out in our lives. Keep believing through it all. Even when you feel defeated, keep your mind stayed on God. He will never let you fall. He has a plan greater than our own. Trust Him to see you through and that everything will work out for your good. The battle has already been fought and won. The victory is yours!

~

Prayer

Lord, thank You for fighting my battles. I trust You to take care of me and see me through whatever I am facing. Grant me peace and the strength to keep standing as You go before me and prepare the way. I know that You are faithful and Your word is true. I am confident that the battle has already been fought and won. Thank You for the victory; In Jesus' Name; Amen.

Scriptures

Romans 8:31

Romans 8:37

2 Corinthians 2:14

Exercise

Claim the victory. See your situation as being resolved. Write down everything you are going through, then cross it out and write resolved. Thank God for the victory.

"For the Lord your God is He that goeth with you, to fight for you against your enemies, to save you.

-Deuteronomy 20: 4 (KJB)

Day 20
Where art Thou?

"Fear not, for I am with you; be not dismayed, for I am your God; I will strengthen you, I will help you, I will uphold you with my righteous right hand."

-*Matthew 28:20 (ESV)*

Doubting that God is with you is like doubting the air around us, yet, we breathe. God is very much present, and even if He isn't tangible, He is visible in the same way that air is visible in a living being. Our living and breathing is visual evidence that air exist, even if we cannot see it. The evidence that God is present lies in the miracles that have occurred in your life and the lives around you. He will never leave or forsake you. He exists in your blessings, answered prayers, solved problems, and all the ways made when there was no way. When you can't feel Him, just look around and refer back to the things He has already done. Even when you cannot see Him, He's there. Breathe and just Believe!

~

Prayer

Lord, thank You for fighting my battles. I trust You to take care of me and see me through whatever I am facing. Grant me peace and the strength to keep standing as You go before me and prepare the way. I know that You are faithful and Your word is true. I am confident that the battle has already been fought and won. Thank You for the victory; In Jesus' Name; Amen.

Scriptures

Deuteronomy 31:6

Joshua 1:9

Psalm 23:4

Exercise

When you feel as though God is not there, put your hand up to your mouth and breathe. Feel the air on your hand and fingers as a reminder that, just like the air, even when we can't see Him, God is there.

"Teaching them to observe all that I have commanded you. And behold, I am with you always, to the end of the age."

-Matthew 28:20 (ESV)

Day 21
Sufficient Grace

"Each time he said, 'My grace is all you need. My power works best in weakness.' So now I am glad to boast about my weaknesses, so that the power of Christ can work through me."

-2 Corinthians 12:9 (NLT)

I used to sit around with a pen in my hand and the tip held against a piece of paper. I did this day in and day out. I was writing down everything I wanted to do, ideas, and anything else I was passionate about. Once I looked them over, I'd get discouraged when I looked around and wondered how I was going to do any of the things I had written without the right resources. Soon after, I'd end up crossing off what I had written, one by one. I'd become so discouraged that I would spiral down into sorrow and gloom as I saw no way out. The problem was that I looked at things from what *I* could do and not what God can do. You have everything you need to succeed. And whatever you cannot do, God can. He has provided you with the necessary tools to carry out your purpose. You can go the distance because His grace is sufficient for each day's tasks. Stay on God's timing and there is no way you can fail. Listen to His guidance and follow His instruction, and grace will guide you to victory! God will provide. Press on!

~

Prayer

Heavenly Father, thank You for always providing a way. Even when I cannot see a solution, You always provide. Help me to keep my eyes on You instead of what I can do alone. Remind me that Your grace is sufficient and that You have already given me everything I need to succeed. With You, I cannot fail; In Jesus' Name; Amen.

Scriptures

Romans 5:1-21

Matthew 6:25-34

Matthew 6:33

Exercise

Start now. Don't look at your resources and what you can do; look at what God can do through you and go forward. He has given you everything you need to succeed. Pray and ask Him to show you the way.

"And my God will supply every need of yours according to His riches in glory in Christ Jesus."

-Philippians 4:19 (ESV)

Day 22
Look Forward to Greater

"Expect great things from God, Attempt great things for God."

-William Carey (1761-1834) Missionary

Things may be so out of whack that it seems as if you'll never accomplish your dream or reach your goals. The situation you're in, right now, may seem as though things won't get better. One of the many good things of God is that He doesn't operate on what seems likely – He operates on His promises, His power, and His timing. Your only job is to believe. It's that difficult and that easy!

~

Prayer

Lord, thank You for being there. Cover me in Your peace while I wait patiently on You to do as You have promised. Shine Your light for me so that I may find my way. Encourage my heart so that I am reminded that You have already gone before me to make a way. Help me to not grow weary while I am waiting and doing as You have instructed. I look forward to greater; In Jesus' Name; Amen.

Scriptures

Galatians 6:9

Psalm 27:14

Isaiah 40:31

Exercise

Keep going. Trust God to do as He has promised. Refuse to grow weary and give up. Pray and ask God to renew your strength. As you look forward to greater, thank God for the blessings that are on the way and what He is doing on your behalf.

"For still the vision awaits its appointed time; it hastens to the end – it will not lie. If it seems slow, wait for it; it will surely come; it will not delay."

-Habakkuk 2:3 (ESV)

Day 23
More Precious than Gold

"They are more precious than gold, than much pure gold; they are sweeter than honey, than honey from the honeycomb."

-Psalm 19:10 (NIV)

You are valuable. Your worth is not defined by your circumstances or anything you've done. God sees you as valuable. Learn to see yourself the way God sees you. Know your worth as defined by God. You are precious in His sight. He values you so much that He sent His only Son into the world to give His life for you. Know that there is nothing you can do to change God's mind about you. Honor yourself and be reminded that you are worthy. The way you treat yourself and the way you allow others to treat you shows how much you value yourself. Take no less than you deserve. You are a child of the King and you are Worthy.

~

Prayer

Dear God, help me to see my worth. Uncover the veil of darkness that overshadows all that You say I am. Remove the barriers that have been placed on me that keep me from seeing my value and worth. I want to be treated the way You intended and nothing less. Remind me that I am more precious than Gold. Help me to see myself the way You see me. Thank You Father; In Jesus' Name; Amen.

Scriptures

Malachi 3:17

Psalm 139:14

Psalm 139:17

Exercise

See yourself the way God sees you. On purpose, remind yourself everyday that you are valuable. Write it down so that you have a constant reminder that you are more precious than gold.

"Since you are precious and honored in my sight, and because I love you, I will give people in exchange for you, nations in exchange for your life."

-Isaiah 43:4 (NIV)

Day 24
Hidden places

"As for me, I will call upon God; and the Lord shall save me."

-Psalm 55:16 (KJB)

There is nowhere you can go that God won't be able to find you. No matter how low life can make you feel, God is well able to reach down and pull you out of your situation at any moment. Trust Him to know where you are at this point in your life and what you need. There is no circumstance that can keep God from getting to you. He will deliver.

~

Prayer

Father, I know that You have plans for me. Give me peace as I wait for You. I believe in Your word and rely on Your promise to never leave or forsake me. Help me to be patient. Renew my strength so that I will not grow weary and give up. Thank You for all that You are doing on my behalf, even now; In Jesus' Name; Amen.

Scriptures

John 14:17

Philippians 4:19

Genesis 22:14

Exercise

Bless someone while you are waiting on God to move in your life. Go out looking for someone you can help. When we focus on meeting the needs of others, it not only pleases God but it causes you to be blessed as you wait.

"For I am about to do something new. See, I have already begun! Do you not see it? I will make a pathway through the wilderness. I will create rivers in the dry wasteland.

-Isaiah 43:19 (NLT)

Day 25
The Treasures of Heaven

"...and see if I do not make the windows of heaven open and send down such a blessing on you that there is no room for it."

-Malachi 3:10 (BEB)

When we give, it not only pleases God but it also causes us to be blessed. Tithing is so important and vital to our lives. Give into the kingdom of God and He will pour out blessings that you do not have room to contain, even pressed down shaken together and running over. He will hold true to His promise to multiply you. And God honors sacrifice. Even if you don't have much to give, there is something you can give. Give your time to serve in a way that honors and blesses God. Use your skills to glorify Him. Whatever you have that you can use to honor God and glorify Him, use it. Whatever you give, do it from the heart and watch God open up the windows of heaven and pour out blessings upon you!

～

Prayer

Dear Lord, bless me to be a blessing. Speak to my heart regarding my giving. Tell me what You want me to do. I may not have much to give, but I want to give my best. Show me what I have that I can use to glorify You and elevate the Kingdom. Multiply me so that I can increase my giving. Thank you Father; In Jesus' Name; Amen.

Scriptures

Malachi 3:10

2 Corinthians 9:7

James 1:17

Exercise

Give your best. Look for ways to bless God with what you have. Pray and believe that God will reveal ways that you can give.

"Give and it shall be given unto you; good measure, pressed down, and shaken together, and running over, shall men give into your bosom. For with the same measure that ye mete withal it shall be measured to you again."

-Luke 6:38 (KJB)

Day 26
Go Out Of Your Way

"Do not neglect to do good and to share what you have, for such sacrifices are pleasing to God."
-Hebrews 13:16 (ESV)

When you go out of your way to help someone else and show compassion, God will in turn go out of His way to show compassion towards you. It pleases God to see you taking care of your brothers and sisters in Christ. It shows Him that you are reliable. And when God can trust you to use what you have and go out of your way to bless someone, He will give you more. He wants to use people who will do the work here on earth. If he knows that He can use you, He will sustain you and multiply you so that you may carry out the mission and show His love. Look for ways to bless someone. Go out of your way to make sure someone else has what they need, and God will surely supply all of your needs.

~

Prayer

Dear Lord, I want to be a cheerful giver. I want to honor You by tending to the needs of others. Bless me so that I may be a blessing to others. Use me Lord. You showed the ultimate sacrificial gift when You gave Your life for me. I want to be more like You Jesus. Touch my heart and multiply every area of my life so that I may be of help to others. Thank you Father; In Jesus' Name; Amen.

Scriptures

Matthew 25:35-40

James 2:14-17

1 John 3:17

Exercise

Show others the love of God by meeting their need. Continue in your giving and going out with the intent to bless someone. As you go out of your way for others, God will go out of His way to bless you. -- *"Whoever is generous to the poor lends to the Lord, and he will repay him for his deed."*   -Proverbs 19:17 (ESV)

"Let each of you look not only to his own interest, but also to the interests of others."
                                    -Philippians 2:4 (ESV)

"Give to the one who begs from you, and do not refuse the one who would borrow from you."
                                    -Matthew 5:42 (ESV)

Day 27
Patience

"For still the vision awaits its appointed time; it hastens to the end—it will not lie. If it seems slow, wait for it; it will surely come; it will not delay."

-Habakkuk 2:3 (ESV)

I used to drive myself insane doing a whole bunch of stuff to get my prayers answered. I took matters into my own hands and tried to make things happen. I was tired of waiting and could no longer stand it. What I learned is that as long as I was moving around trying to make things happen, God wasn't going to touch it. He was waiting for me to let go and let God. When I finally let go and surrendered to God and where He had me, I saw things turn around almost immediately. Know that God's timing is perfect. He knows everything that we want Him to do in our lives, and He wants to do better than that. When you become anxious and start to move ahead of God, pray and ask Him to give you peace. Surrender and trust that He has gone before you to do what only He can do. It is just a matter of time before you see the manifestation of His finished work!

~

Prayer

Father, ease my mind and calm my spirit. Forgive me for becoming anxious and moving ahead of You. I know that Your timing is perfect, and at the appointed time, You will move on my behalf. Thank You for the blessings that are yet to come and all of the prayers that You have answered. You have always been there for me. Thank You for the promise to never leave or forsake me. As it says in Your word that You will grant the desires of my heart. I trust You Lord. You know when and what is best for me; In Jesus' Name; Amen.

Scriptures

Isaiah 40:31

Ecclesiastes 8:6

Psalm 27:14

Exercise

Thank God while you wait. Write down something everyday that you are thankful for. Thank Him for them all.

"And let us not grow weary of doing good, for in due season we will reap, if we do not give up."
-Galatians 6:9 (ESV)

"Trust in the Lord with all your heart, and do not lean on your own understanding. In all your ways acknowledge him, and he will make straight your paths."
-Proverbs 3:5-6 (ESV)

Day 28
Pride – the Blessing Killer

"One's pride will bring him low, but he who is lowly in spirit will obtain honor."

-Proverbs 29:23 (ESV)

My grandfather was one who would never ask for help. No matter how much trouble he was in or how difficult a situation, he would suffer rather than ask for help. Even if there was someone who could help him and they were willing, he wouldn't hear of it. He'd starve before asking anyone for a handout. I used to sit there, starving, wondering why he wouldn't ask someone for help. He'd get angry every time I brought up someone who wanted to help. As I grew older, I found myself having a hard time asking for help when I needed it. I didn't want anyone thinking I was needy when I actually was. Like my grandfather, I wanted to appear as though I had it all together – when everything was falling apart. When I realized that these habits were hurting me, I quickly prayed for a change. God cannot bless us when we are full of pride. Whether it's asking for forgiveness or asking for food, God wants us to be humble. Through prayer and obedience to His word, I overcame pride and gained a humble heart. Refuse to let pride still your blessings.

~

Prayer

Lord, change my heart. Erase all traces of pride that hinder my blessings and destroy my elevation. I want to be pleasing in Your site. Show me how to submit and be humble. Help me to know when I am being prideful so that I may correct my mistakes. I want to be more like You Lord. Forgive me for allowing pride to enter my life. I submit to You Lord to have Your way with me. Thank You Father; In Jesus' Name; Amen.

Scriptures

Galatians 6:3

Proverbs 16:5

Proverbs 16:18

Exercise

Practice humility. Ask someone for help--Be the first to apologize to someone even if you feel it was there fault. Show God that you want to be humble.

"But he gives more grace. Therefore it says, 'God opposes the proud, but gives grace to the humble.'"
                                        -James 4:6 (ESV)

"When pride comes, then comes disgrace, but with the humble is wisdom."
                                        -Proverbs 11:2 (ESV)

Day 29
Armor

"For the word of God is alive and powerful. It is sharper than the sharpest two-edged sword, cutting between soul and spirit, between joint and marrow. It exposes our innermost thoughts and desires."

-Hebrews 4:12 (NLT)

When I became lazy and stopped studying the word of God, I felt worn out and defeated. I thought that I could weather the storms by myself without the word of God to protect me. Whenever I faced a battle, I felt defeated almost instantly. At first, I had no clue why I seemed to be getting hit harder than I ever had by life's circumstances. It wasn't until I was pushed back into the word by a drastic situation that I discovered a renewing of my strength. I knew right then that there was no way I could live without the word of God covering me when I was going through. Also, the word of God helped me live a better life and warned me against situations that I would have walked into had it not been for it. Guidance and protection under the word is available to anyone who will seek it. Picking up the word keeps us well equipped to deal with the situations that may arise in life. When you digest the word of God, you become equipped with enough power to go through any situation. Study the word often and remember to keep God and His word first place!

~

Prayer

Father, thank You for Your word. Your guidance lies between the covers of the holy book. The words on those pages are alive and are at work in my life when I digest them. Give me godly wisdom and knowledge so that I may understand what I am reading when I study the word, and that I may apply it to my everyday life. Allow it to penetrate my heart and my spirit so that I may be renewed. As I study Your word, I pray that there is a renewing of my mind so that I can live under Your divine protection and be better equipped to endure any situation that may arise; In Jesus' Name; Amen.

Scriptures

Jeremiah 23:29

2 Timothy 3:16-17

Ephesians 6:17

Exercise

Make an appointment everyday to study the word of God. Even if it's just a scripture for 15 minutes per day, make it a part of your regular schedule.

"But he answered and said, It is written, Man shall not live by bread alone, but by every word that proceedeth out of the mouth of God."

-Matthew 4:4 (KJB)

Day 30
If God is For You

"What then shall we say to these things? If God is for us, who can be against us?"

-Romans 8:31 (ESV)

If God is for us, who can be against us? God is rooting for you. He wants to see you succeed. His vision for you is that you become everything He ever knew you could be. When you start realizing that the creator of the universe is there to catch you when you fall and carry you when you are weak, you will begin to live a life that was once only a dream. You cannot fail when there is a God residing in you that cannot fail. Step out of the boat and move away from your comfort zone and allow God to have His way in your life. Everything you want in this life is obtainable through God. There is no one and no situation that can keep God from seeing you through. God will open doors for you that no one can shut – doors that you are not qualified to walk into. And He will sustain you. You have the almighty Savior on your side, and if He is for you, no one can be against you!

~

Prayer

Heavenly Father, thank You for always being there for me. Thank You for making a way for me. I know that if You are for me, there is no one that can be against me. Your word is true and I trust in You alone to see me through. I know that there is nothing that You wouldn't do for me. Give me the courage to step out of my comfort zone and walk on water. I want to step out on faith and live the life You created me to live and be the person You created me to be. I want to live my life the way You see it in Your eyes. I know that with You Lord, I cannot fail; In Jesus' Name; Amen.

Scriptures

2 Timothy 2:13

Deuteronomy 31:6

Joshua 1:9

Exercise

What would you do or become if you knew that there was no way you could fail? Know that God is with you. Go on and pursue everything God put in your heart to do or become. He is with you. Victory is already yours!

"Fear not, for I am with you; be not dismayed, for I am your God; I will strengthen you, I will help you, I will uphold you with my righteous right hand."

-Isaiah 41:10 (ESV)

www.ingramcontent.com/pod-product-compliance
Lightning Source LLC
Chambersburg PA
CBHW060537030426
42337CB00021B/4315